Bless my Soul

Patrice Rutty

Presentation by *BookLeaf Publishing*

Web: www.bookleafpub.com

E-mail: info@bookleafpub.com

ISBN: 9789360946562

First edition 2024

This book is dedicated to my children Bless, Ashanti, Tsion, Zaire, Londyn, Royal, Reign and my God daughter Jenea. As you journey through life, may these pages serve as a source of inspiration, guiding you toward your dreams and empowering you to embrace the magic that resides within your souls.

May you always remember the strength and resilience that flows through your veins, the beauty that radiates from your hearts, and the wisdom that resides in the depths of your spirits. Know that no matter where life may lead you, you have the power to make this world a better place. Always be kind!

With all my love unconditionally,

Mama

ACKNOWLEDGEMENT

I am grateful to my children for their patience with me, mentors and teachers whose words have ignited the flames of inspiration within me. Your wisdom has been a guiding light, illuminating the path of self-discovery and personal growth.

I extend my deepest gratitude to the publishing team at Book Leaf whose dedication and expertise have brought this book to life. Your passion for sharing stories of hope and transformation has been instrumental in bringing this project to fruition.

Last but certainly not least, I express my heartfelt appreciation to you, reader. It is through your openness and willingness to embark on this journey that the true magic of inspiration unfolds. May the words within these pages serve as a guiding light on your path toward fulfillment and self-discovery.

With boundless gratitude,
Patrice

PREFACE

Welcome to the beginning of a transformational journey. In the pages that follow, you'll find a collection of thoughts and insights written to ignite the fire of inspiration within you. This book is not merely ink on paper; it's a beacon of light, guiding you and empowering you to rise above any challenge.

Inspiration is not a destination; it's a constant companion on the path of life. It whispers in the wind, dances in the sunlight, and resides within the depths of your being, waiting to be unleashed. As you immerse yourself in the words that follow, may you be reminded of the boundless potential that lives within you and I hope you find the courage to pursue your dreams with unwavering determination.

So, let us embark on this journey together, with open hearts and open minds, ready to embrace the infinite possibilities that lie ahead. For within the pages of this book, lies the power to transform not only your life but the world around you.

Practice Meditation

Meditation is indeed a powerful tool for nurturing the mind and spirit, fostering clarity and inner peace amidst the chaos of life. By dedicating time to sit in stillness, focusing on the rhythm of our breath, we create space for tranquility to permeate our being.

Through regular practice, we invite profound transformation into our lives. The benefits extend far beyond mere stress reduction and improved focus; meditation has the profound ability to reshape our entire perspective on life. It teaches us to observe our thoughts without attachment, to cultivate compassion and understanding in our relationships, and to navigate the ebb and flow of existence with grace and resilience.

Yet, amidst the serenity of meditation, it's important to remember that life continues outside the realm of our thoughts. While getting lost in positive contemplation can be uplifting, it's essential to recognize that challenges and difficulties will inevitably arise. Meditation does not exempt us from the realities of life, but it equips us with the inner strength and clarity to face them with courage and grace.

So, as you embark on your meditation journey, remember that the true essence of the practice lies not in escaping reality, but in embracing it fully, with an open heart and a tranquil mind. Through the simple act of sitting and breathing, you'll discover a profound sense of stillness and peace that resides within you, waiting to be awakened.

Committing to a daily practice, even just 10 to 15 minutes a day, is an act of self-love and discipline. It is a sacred commitment to our own well-being, a recognition of our inherent worthiness of peace and tranquility. By carving out this time each day, we honor ourselves and our journey toward inner transformation.

Consistency is key in building a meditation practice. By establishing a dedicated time and space for meditation, we create a ritual that nourishes our spirit and fosters growth. Proper posture, with a straight back and relaxed neck, allows for optimal alignment of body and mind, facilitating a deeper connection to the present moment.

Commit to this practice with dedication and devotion, knowing that in doing so, you are paving the way for a healthier, happier, and more fulfilling life.

Resiliency

Embrace challenges as opportunities for growth. Cultivate resilience by adopting a positive mindset and learning from setbacks. Remember that you have the strength to overcome any obstacles that come your way.Let your struggles be your motivation, Don't allow your struggles to hold you down and cause you to live your life in fear of rising and keep you from all the beautiful and amazing things that's manifested for you. Mentally we have to be stronger than how we physically feel. Everything in creation struggles. The trees don't choose when they get water. It always has to wait for the rain to fall.Things happen in life that makes us sad or can even be a setback. Sometimes it's just that random test we have to pass. It's important how we choose to handle those situations. Do we sit in perpetual sadness or we can choose to rise above our situation and treasure our most precious gift which is life. Never forget about the bigger picture. We tend to focus on the minor things and not the major things that are important in our lives. If we continue to focus on the negative setbacks we won't see our full potential. Live with a positive mindset even

when things don't seem to be as bright or
promising as you would want them to be. Have
faith in what will be regardless of the current
status. We all have great inner power but
acknowledging inner peace is the first way to
conquer. That inner peace is self faith. Worrying
doesn't change anything. It only slows down our
process of overcoming.
Be strong and courageous. Turn every negative
into something positive. The only reason we
were given this life is because we are strong
enough to live it.

Self Love and Self Care

Living life to the fullest means embracing positivity and indulging in activities that bring us joy and fulfillment. Whether it's snapping a selfie, treating ourselves to a shopping spree, or exploring new places, it's essential to prioritize self-care and nourish our souls with the things we love. Prioritize self-care and make time for activities that nourish your body, mind, and spirit. This could include exercise, healthy eating, pampering yourself, or simply taking a relaxing bath.

Self-love lies at the heart of our well-being, reminding us of our inherent worthiness and deservingness of happiness. It's about honoring our true selves, embracing our flaws and imperfections, and treating ourselves with the kindness and compassion we so freely extend to others.

Self-love is not selfish; it's a profound act of self-preservation and empowerment. By nurturing our inner selves, we cultivate greater self-esteem, resilience, and inner stability, empowering us to navigate life's challenges with grace and confidence.

When we love ourselves deeply, we radiate a positive energy that attracts like-minded souls into our lives—individuals who value and appreciate us for who we are. Our self-perception sets the tone for the relationships we cultivate and the standards we set for ourselves and others.

Ultimately, self-love is the cornerstone of a fulfilling and meaningful existence. It empowers us to live authentically, to pursue our dreams with unwavering determination, and to embrace the fullness of life with open hearts and minds. So, let us embrace self-love wholeheartedly, for it is the greatest gift we can give ourselves and the world around us.

Acceptance

Acceptance is the cornerstone of living a fulfilling and meaningful life. It's about embracing the present moment with open arms, acknowledging that everything unfolds in its own time and according to its own purpose.

Life becomes infinitely easier when we learn to accept the things we cannot change. It's about working with what the present moment offers, even when options seem limited or situations seem challenging. Strength lies in our ability to face adversity head-on, with courage and resilience, trusting that even in the midst of uncertainty, there is a lesson to be learned and growth to be gained.

Hope is an ever-present beacon, guiding us through the darkest of times and reminding us that negative situations can be transformed into positive outcomes. It's through the acceptance of life's ebb and flow that we discover the true essence of happiness and fulfillment.

Understanding the balance of life allows us to accept the inevitability of change and the transient nature of our circumstances. By being realistic and embracing the present moment, we free ourselves from the burden of unrealistic expectations and open ourselves up to the endless possibilities that lie ahead.

In the face of life's pressures, it's crucial to find peace and solace, knowing that we are not alone in our journey. Trusting in a higher power, whether it be called God or by another name, provides us with the strength and resilience to weather life's storms and navigate its twists and turns with grace and dignity.

Ultimately, it's about letting go of our attachments to how we think things should be and surrendering to the beauty of what is. While we may plan and strive for certain outcomes, it is the universe, or a higher power, that holds the ultimate plan—a plan that is often far more wondrous and intricate than anything we could have imagined.

Purpose

You were born to shine brightly, to illuminate the world with the unique brilliance of your being. Stop trying to conform to the expectations of others and instead embrace the divine essence that sets you apart. Your presence in this world is not mere chance; it is a testament to the divine purpose that flows through your veins.

Your purpose is the compass that guides you toward a life of fulfillment and meaning. It is the driving force behind your actions, passions, and talents, leading you on a journey of self-discovery and contribution to the greater good. When you align with your purpose, you unlock the door to a life filled with joy, abundance, and significance.

Life is not meant to be lived in isolation; it is meant to be shared and celebrated with others. When you live with purpose, you become a beacon of inspiration, touching the lives of those around you and leaving an indelible mark on the world.

Discovering your purpose is a sacred journey, a process of deep introspection and alignment with your innermost truths. It is not dictated by external factors such as wealth, status, or societal norms, but rather by the calling of your heart and the whispers of your soul.

Your purpose is your truth, and it requires courage and faith to embrace it fully. It may demand that you step out of your comfort zone, take risks, and trust in the divine guidance that resides within you. But know that when you walk in alignment with your purpose, you walk in harmony with the universe, and miracles unfold with each step you take.

So, my love, embrace your purpose with open arms, for it is the key to unlocking the full potential of your being and living a life of profound meaning and fulfillment. Trust in the journey, and let your purpose be your guiding light through the darkest of nights and the brightest of days.

A leap of Faith

The greatest transformation we can experience is found in taking a leap of faith. It's about trusting in the unseen, stepping out into the unknown with courage and conviction.

Faith is the cornerstone of our journey, the unwavering belief that propels us forward even when the path ahead seems uncertain. It's about having confidence in the face of adversity, knowing that we are guided and supported by a higher power.

When we have faith, we possess a sense of assurance and comfort that transcends the limitations of our physical reality. It's the substance of our hopes and dreams, the driving force behind our aspirations and desires.

Faith is a gift bestowed upon us by the divine, a testament to the power of belief and trust in the universe. It's through the examples of faith found in the scriptures and the teachings of spiritual leaders that our own faith is strengthened and nourished.

In the grand scheme of things, faith is the currency of the soul, the currency that unlocks the gates of greatness and abundance. It's through our unwavering belief in ourselves and in the divine plan that we manifest miracles and overcome seemingly insurmountable obstacles.

But faith requires a single-minded focus, a commitment to listening with our hearts and following the guidance of the divine. With faith as our compass, we spread our wings and soar to new heights, knowing that with God's guidance, no obstacle is too great to overcome.

So let us embrace the transforming power of faith, knowing that with each step we take in faith, we move closer to our divine purpose and the fulfillment of our deepest desires. Trust in the journey, and watch as miracles unfold before your eyes.

Love intentionally

To Love truly is the most powerful force in the universe, a seed planted by the divine and nurtured by our own actions and intentions. It has the miraculous ability to transform the darkest hours into the most vibrant moments,

Love is not merely a feeling; it is a conscious choice and a deliberate action. It's about extending kindness, compassion, and empathy to all beings, regardless of their circumstances or actions. When we love without expectation or condition, we tap into the infinite wellspring of love that flows from the depths of our souls.

We were created to love, for we are born from love itself. It is our inherent nature to love and be loved in return. Love is not only beneficial for our emotional well-being but also for our physical health, as it has been shown to reduce stress, boost immunity, and promote longevity.

In the presence of love, fear dissipates, replaced by hope, joy, and inspiration. Unconditional love respects boundaries, honors differences, and gives freely without expectation of reciprocity. It is through acts of kindness, forgiveness, and generosity that we create a world filled with love and compassion.

By practicing random acts of kindness, offering a smile or a listening ear, and extending a helping hand to those in need, we contribute to the collective expansion of love in the world. Love knows no limitations or boundaries; it transcends all barriers and unites us in a bond of shared humanity.

So, let us love fearlessly and unconditionally, for in doing so, we not only uplift and inspire others but also cultivate a sense of profound fulfillment and purpose within ourselves. Love is the greatest gift we can give to the world, and it is through love that we truly make a difference in the lives of others and in the world at large.

Self Control

In order to cultivate self-control, one must first recognize its value. A lack of self-control leaves one vulnerable, similar to a city with crumbling walls, prone to collapse at any moment. Self-control is not natural to a person or thing, rather it is learned or acquired through experience. It is a skill to be honed. It signifies being guided by principles. Self-control is synonymous with willpower, the force that enables us to steer our actions towards virtuous decisions. At its core lies discipline, demanding both physical and mental exertion to refine oneself. Mastering self-control necessitates the removal of temptations, allowing clarity and resolve to flourish.

Self-control is a crucial skill for achieving success in various aspects of life, including health, relationships, work, and personal development. It requires discipline, willpower, and the ability to manage impulses effectively. Strategies for enhancing self-control include setting clear goals, practicing mindfulness and self-awareness, developing healthy habits, and utilizing techniques such as cognitive restructuring and delayed gratification.

Patience

A waiting person embodies patience. Patience entails the willingness to remain in a situation, trusting that hidden opportunities will reveal themselves in due time. It's a learned attitude cultivated through acceptance, even amidst adversity. Every instance of patience holds a valuable lesson. Patience is not passive; rather, it's a potent form of resilience and compassion. It involves embracing the uncertainty of life and understanding that progress may not always be immediate.

The wisdom in the quote, 'So don't be anxious about tomorrow. God will take care of your tomorrow too. Live one day at a time,' underscores the power of living in the present moment. Surrendering to impatience only breeds frustration and does little to alter circumstances. Instead, patience empowers us to endure, confident that our moment will arrive in due course."
It involves having the willingness to accept delays, uncertainties, and setbacks while persevering towards one's goals with a sense of tranquility and trust in the process. Patience is

not merely passive waiting but an active practice of resilience, self-discipline, and faith in the eventual fruition of our efforts. It allows us to navigate life's uncertainties with grace and fortitude, knowing that every moment of waiting holds the potential for growth, learning, and eventual fulfillment.

Love now

The best time to love is always now. Love is the greatest gift we can offer ourselves or others in life. It embodies gentleness, kindness, patience, forgiveness, compassion, charity, and humility. Love permeates every aspect of existence. Since tomorrow is not promised, seizing the opportunity to love in the present moment is paramount. Let go of bitterness, hatred, and malice, and embrace the transformative power of love without regret.

Never hesitate to express your love to others, for time is fleeting and uncertain. True love does not inflict pain, betray trust, enslave, or disappoint; instead, it liberates and uplifts. Loving in the present requires no prerequisites or effort; it is enough in itself. The more love we give, the more we receive, opening pathways to unforeseen experiences and connections. Ultimately, love is a fundamental aspect of the human experience, shaping our relationships, attitudes, and sense of belonging in the world. Love transcends superficial feelings; it is a spiritual force that both heals and empowers. Embracing love requires courage, yet true love knows no boundaries. Without love, life loses its brightness. There is no need to wait for a more opportune time, for in the now, love finds its truest expression. It is in this moment that we can extend a hand of kindness, offer a word of encouragement, or share a heartfelt embrace. seize this moment, for it is the best time to love, to cherish, and to be present with all our hearts. Seize this moment, for it is the best time to love, to cherish, and to be present with all our hearts.

Principles of your thoughts and your Words

Two essential principles to bear in mind in life:

Take care of your thoughts when you are alone. Mind your words when you are with others.

While thoughts may seem intangible, they wield significant power. They can either nurture or harm. Our thoughts possess the potential to shape the life we desire. What we consistently focus on or dwell upon determines our direction. We are, in essence, the culmination of our thoughts, which play a crucial role in shaping our destiny.

Similarly, exercise caution with your words. The tongue has the capacity to inflict wounds far deeper than any physical weapon."

Words can be a tool without physical force, yet possessing immense power. They can ignite flames without fuel, lighting up a house with mere breath. They hold no physical weight, but their impact can be heavy, sparking conflicts and wars. The tongue, though soft, can be harsh, inflicting great damage and pain. Yet, it also has the potential to create better experiences and build up others. Let us set rules for our tongues, using them to speak truth and kindness. Let our words be filled with blessings, encouragement, praise, and wisdom. Practice self-control, for the tongue can control us if we let it. As Proverbs 50 verse four reminds us, a healing tongue is a tree of life, while a deceitful one crushes the spirit.

Words hold the potential to shape relationships, influence perceptions, and leave lasting impacts. Whether spoken in moments of anger, joy, or indifference, words carry weight beyond measure. They can build bridges of understanding or erect walls of division. Like arrows released from a bow, once spoken, words cannot be easily retracted. Therefore, let us choose our words thoughtfully, with empathy and respect, mindful of their impact on others and the world around us.

Stop Complaining

It's easy to get caught up in complaining, but it's essential to remember that there's always someone out there facing much greater challenges.

Let's shift our focus towards appreciation and thankfulness. Complaining drains our energy and heightens our stress levels, creating a cycle of negativity and anxiety. Instead, let's work on breaking the habit of complaining and embrace a more positive outlook.

Here are some practical ways to help stop complaining:

Implement a "no complain" diet.
1. Surround yourself with people who have a positive mindset.
2. Take proactive steps to resolve any issues you encounter.
3. Regularly count your blessings and practice gratitude.
4. By making these changes, we can experience a newfound energy and greater happiness in our lives.

Potential

You were destined for greatness, so don't confine yourself to small aspirations. Give yourself permission to live a life of significance and purpose. Step into the fullness of who you are meant to be and inspire others along the way. Don't wait for external inspiration; instead, ignite the fire within yourself. Refuse to settle for mediocrity; always strive for more, for you were born to achieve greatness. Recognize your inherent value and refuse to diminish it. Stand out, make lasting impressions, and have unwavering faith in your dreams. You were created for a purpose, and it's time to embrace your destiny with confidence and determination.

Forgiveness

Forgiveness is a powerful tool for healing, helping us shed the burden of resentment and anger. It's essential to cultivate the capacity to forgive, both for our own well-being and for the betterment of our relationships. True love involves not only forgiving others but also allowing ourselves to be forgiven.

In every person, there is both good and evil, and forgiveness is the intentional process of releasing negative emotions such as vengefulness. Sometimes, our reluctance to forgive stems from a lack of understanding about its nature. We may fear that by forgiving, we are letting the wrongdoer off the hook while we continue to suffer.

However, forgiveness is not about absolving others of responsibility or condoning their actions. Rather, it's about releasing ourselves from the burden of bitterness and resentment. We can still hold others accountable for their behavior while choosing to forgive them.

Forgiveness is a personal journey, and it doesn't always require informing the other person. It's about shifting our attitude and mindset, allowing ourselves to move forward without carrying the weight of past grievances.

Forgiveness does not mean forgetting; memories may resurface, but it's how we choose to respond to them that matters. Instead of dwelling on the past, we can use these reminders as opportunities to reaffirm our commitment to forgiveness and gratitude. Ultimately, forgiveness is about reclaiming our peace and allowing ourselves to let go and move on.

Manifest your best life

Manifesting your best life is a deeply personal journey. At times, life may seem stagnant, but it's crucial to recognize the power of our thoughts and intentions in shaping our reality. Negative thoughts can hinder manifestation, so it's essential to shift our focus towards positivity and clarity.

Free yourself from anything that impedes your belief in your own greatness. Take charge of your life now, aligning your desires with actionable steps towards them. Cultivate confidence and faith in your abilities, visualizing your goals becoming a reality each day.

Yoga and meditation can enhance your manifestation practice by fostering focus and clarity. Stay focused on the desired outcomes, trusting in the universe's timing and process. Release any doubts and fears, allowing your desires to flow effortlessly into the universe.

Work with the universe by being intentional every day about the direction you want your life to take. Align your behaviors with your aspirations, practice positive affirmations, and cultivate gratitude. Instead of feeling envious, let the success of others inspire you on your journey.

Stay Committed & Persistent

When you're committed, nothing can hinder your progress; you persist despite obstacles. Consider the resilience of a plant growing from concrete or a wooden structure devoid of soil—it perseveres regardless. Commitment is about showing up consistently, regardless of motivation or circumstance. Tough times will inevitably arise, but commitment sustains us through them, yielding long-term results. Stay motivated in your commitments; invest your time and belief wholeheartedly. Make firm promises and decisions to honor them. Motivation may drive you initially, but it's commitment that sustains your journey. It forms the foundation of greatness; without it, progress stalls. Remember, partial commitment yields incomplete results; strive for unwavering dedication in all you pursue.

Persistence is key; when you find yourself facing challenges, keep moving forward. Successful individuals don't give up; they persevere through mistakes and setbacks. Remember the words of Conrad Hilton: "When you find yourself in a difficult situation and giving up seems to be the easiest way, remember your why." Surround yourself with accomplished individuals and let their success inspire you to push harder towards your own dreams. Stay focused and avoid distractions, channeling your energy into progress. In times when external motivation is lacking, become your own biggest cheerleader. Be determined, encourage yourself, and never lose sight of your goals. The path to success is paved with persistence; failure is just a stepping stone on the journey. Embrace persistence, turn failures into accomplishments, and keep striving towards your success.

Happiness

Happiness is a choice—a product of my own accomplishments and the blessings I've received. No external force controls my happiness; it emanates from within. True happiness is vital for both emotional and physical well-being; it fosters contentment, enhances relationships, and enriches lives. It's not something inherited but rather a result of our thoughts and actions. Happiness is among the most valuable possessions we can own, yet it can be challenging to maintain over time.

Taking responsibility for our happiness involves engaging in self-care routines, nurturing relationships with loved ones, and pursuing activities that bring joy. Whether it's cooking, hobbies, or simply spending time with family, finding moments of joy is essential. Keeping a gratitude journal, practicing mindfulness, and focusing on the present can also contribute to our happiness.

Even small adjustments can have a significant impact on our overall happiness and well-being. Prioritizing happiness not only improves our mood but also has tangible benefits such as reducing anxiety, alleviating depression, boosting the immune system, and enhancing self-esteem.

Ultimately, happiness is a state of mind that we create for ourselves. By choosing to focus on the positive aspects of life and pursuing our dreams and goals, we can cultivate a lasting sense of happiness and fulfillment. Let's always strive to see the brighter side of ourselves and embrace the joy that surrounds us.

Evolve and Grow

Never believe you're too old to evolve. Take a leap of faith and discover the amazing potential within you. You hold immense power as a human being. Embrace confidence and self-love to transcend the ordinary and free yourself from past pains. You are incredible just as you are today, and you have the capacity to become even better. Don't let the opinions of others dictate your path; focus on your journey towards success and personal growth. Time is precious, so live a life that leaves a positive mark on humanity. Stand up, believe in yourself, and start living."

Cherish Moments

Here's a reminder to cherish each other. This is a important call to action. Let's prioritize how we treat others. Humans desire comfort, support, and kindness, nurturing our relationships through quality time together. Love should be the cornerstone of every day, guiding us through all seasons and uncertainties. Life's unpredictability underscores the importance of checking in on our loved ones and making the most of our time together. This prevents us from living with regrets and having unanswered questions.

As we navigate life's journey, it's crucial to respect differences and always strive for the best for those around us. Time is fleeting, and our presence on this earth is finite. Live with purpose. Let's pursue our dreams with fervor, seizing every opportunity to live life to the fullest. Embrace joy, laughter, and love, and engage in activities that bring happiness and fulfillment. Let's savor every moment, for each instant is a precious gift to be treasured.

Stay Focused

Stay focused; ignore the noise. Don't get distracted! Direct your attention and time to a limited set of priorities. Learn to say no to distractions outside your focus area. You don't have to accept every favor; saying yes can derail your priorities and lead to loss of focus. Be wary of the "helper syndrome"; stick to your decisions. You can't stay focused without good intentions.

Focusing on one task at a time helps you accomplish important things. Avoid wasting time in indecision. Sometimes, disconnect from distractions like Wi-Fi, phones, or browsers to allow ideas to flow. Jot them down, but remember to stay disciplined in your practice. Concentrate on building a solid foundation where you're in control.

Gratitude

The feeling that prompts us to say 'thank you' is powerful. Give thanks for everything, even the struggles that bring forth opportunities. Let not a sunrise or sunset pass without notice, and at day's end, excel and express gratitude for it all. Life manifests in myriad ways, evoking diverse emotions. Gratitude, this attitude of thankfulness, holds immense power. Be thankful for the joys that uplift us and the challenges that shape us. Appreciate the earth and its abundant provisions. It's easy to feel grateful when life is smooth, but maintaining that gratitude amidst hardship and struggle is transformational. Gratitude has the power to energize, heal, and instill hope. Be grateful in all things.